GW01157867

TATE DIARY
2019

Edward Coley Burne-Jones *Summer Snow, engraved by the Dalziel Brothers* published 1863 (detail) Wood engraving on paper 14.6 x 10.8 cm Tate. Presented by Harold Hartley 1925

TATE GENERAL INFORMATION

Tate is a family of four galleries: Tate Britain and Tate Modern in London, Tate Liverpool and Tate St Ives. Each features a particular area of the Tate collection. Tate Britain shows British art from 1500 to the present day, including the Turner Bequest. Tate Modern displays international modern art from 1900 to the present day. Tate Liverpool shows selections of modern and international contemporary art, while Tate St Ives displays works by the St Ives School in the context in which they were created, as well as international modern and contemporary art.

The collection consists of painting, sculpture, installation works and large numbers of watercolours, drawings and modern prints. Artists in the collection include Hogarth, Turner, Constable, Rossetti, Matisse, Picasso, Giacometti, Hepworth, Rothko, Dalí, Bacon, Pollock, Warhol, Riley, Hockney, Hirst and many others.

EVENTS
All four galleries offer a full programme of talks, courses, films and events for adults, young people and families relating to the collection and to exhibitions and displays.

INFORMATION
Visit www.tate.org.uk for details of exhibitions, displays and events. For information on Tate Britain and Tate Modern call 020 7887 8888; on Tate Liverpool, 0151 702 7400; and on Tate St Ives, 01736 796226.

DISABLED VISITORS
Tate welcomes people with disabilities. A number of wheelchairs are available at each gallery and there is lift access in all four galleries. If you would like further information, call the appropriate number given above.

TATE PUBLISHING
A books catalogue is available on request from Tate Enterprises, Millbank, London SW1P 4RG, or by telephoning 020 7887 8869. For more information on our titles visit www.tate.org.uk/publishing.

TATE SHOPS
Tate Shops offer a wide range of books, posters, cards and merchandise related to Tate, the collection and exhibitions. For online purchases visit www.shop.tate.org.uk.

TATE CAFÉS AND RESTAURANTS
All four galleries offer an excellent choice of light meals, snacks and drinks. Tate Britain's Rex Whistler restaurant has an à la carte menu, a set daily menu and a fine wine list.
For reservations call 020 7887 8825 and for the Tate Modern restaurant call 020 7887 8888.

TATE MEMBERS
Support Tate and become a Member to enjoy:
- Unlimited free entry to all Tate exhibtions
- Exclusive access to Members Rooms at Tate Britain and Tate Modern
- Regular listings guides and TATE ETC magazine to your door
- Special viewings opportunities and fast-track exhibtion entry

Your support will help acquire works of art for the collection and provide vital funding for Tate's exciting programme, so you'll be shaping the Tate of the future.

Join in the gallery, online at tate.org.uk/members or call 020 7887 8888.

2019 PUBLIC HOLIDAYS

UNITED KINGDOM	
New Year's Day	1 January
NYD Bank Holiday (Scotland only)	2 January
St Patrick's Day (N.I only)	17 March
St Patrick's Day Bank Holiday (N.I. only)	18 March
Good Friday	19 April
Easter Monday	22 April
Early May Bank Holiday	6 May
Spring Bank Holiday	27 May
Public Holiday (N.I. only)	12 July
Summer Bank Holiday (Scotland only)	5 August
Summer Bank Holiday	26 August
Christmas Day	25 December
Boxing Day	26 December

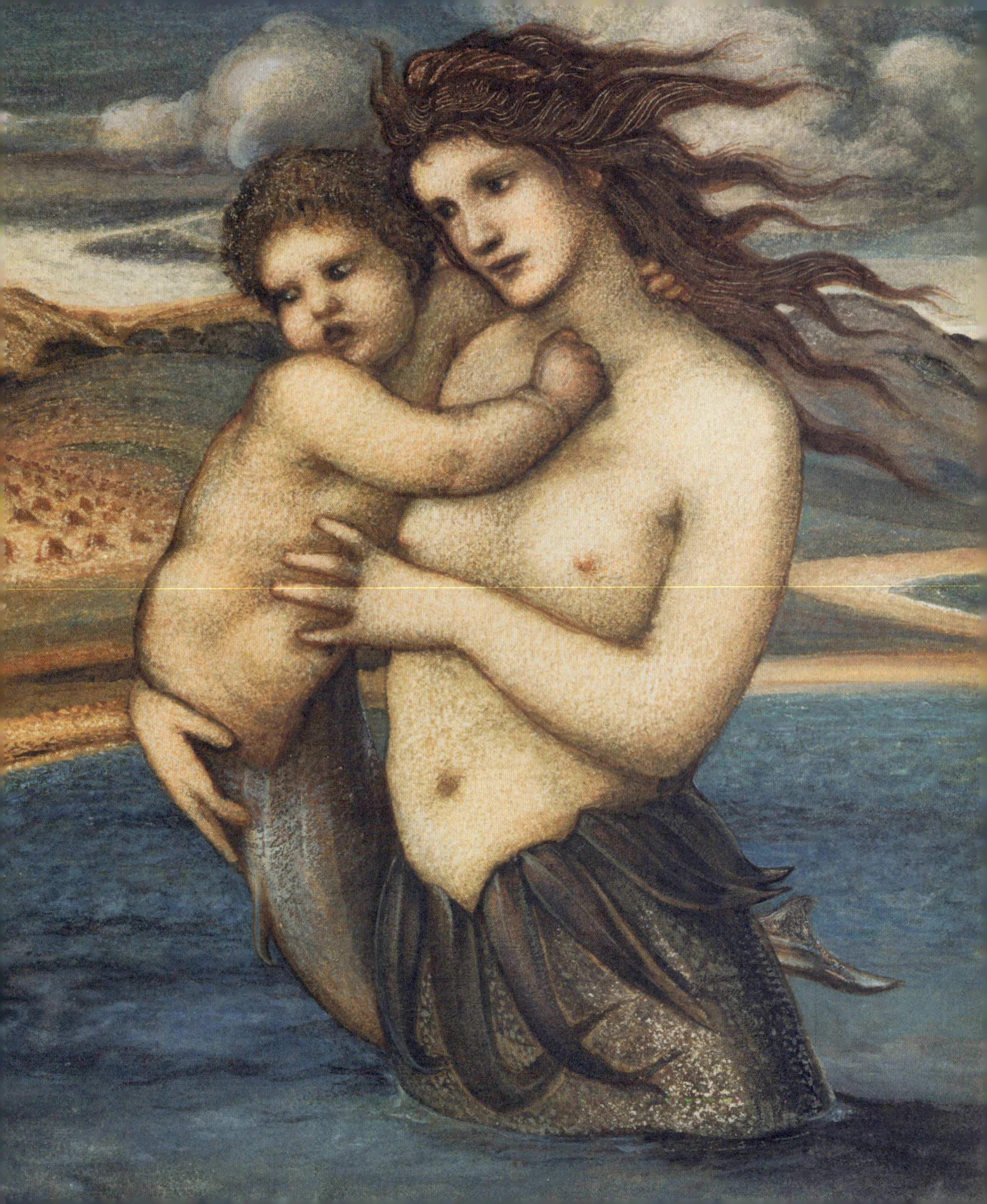

2019

JANUARY
Monday			7	14	21	28
Tuesday		1	8	15	22	29
Wednesday		2	9	16	23	30
Thursday		3	10	17	24	31
Friday		4	11	18	25	
Saturday		5	12	19	26	
Sunday		6	13	20	27	

FEBRUARY
Monday		4	11	18	25
Tuesday		5	12	19	26
Wednesday		6	13	20	27
Thursday		7	14	21	28
Friday	1	8	15	22	
Saturday	2	9	16	23	
Sunday	3	10	17	24	

MARCH
Monday		4	11	18	25	
Tuesday		5	12	19	26	
Wednesday		6	13	20	27	
Thursday		7	14	21	28	
Friday	1	8	15	22	29	
Saturday	2	9	16	23	30	
Sunday	3	10	17	24	31	

APRIL
Monday		1	8	15	22	29
Tuesday		2	9	16	23	30
Wednesday		3	10	17	24	
Thursday		4	11	18	25	
Friday		5	12	19	26	
Saturday		6	13	20	27	
Sunday		7	14	21	28	

MAY
Monday			6	13	20	27
Tuesday			7	14	21	28
Wednesday		1	8	15	22	29
Thursday		2	9	16	23	30
Friday		3	10	17	24	31
Saturday		4	11	18	25	
Sunday		5	12	19	26	

JUNE
Monday		3	10	17	24
Tuesday		4	11	18	25
Wednesday		5	12	19	26
Thursday		6	13	20	27
Friday		7	14	21	28
Saturday	1	8	15	22	29
Sunday	2	9	16	23	30

JULY
Monday	1	8	15	22	29
Tuesday	2	9	16	23	30
Wednesday	3	10	17	24	31
Thursday	4	11	18	25	
Friday	5	12	19	26	
Saturday	6	13	20	27	
Sunday	7	14	21	28	

AUGUST
Monday		5	12	19	26
Tuesday		6	13	20	27
Wednesday		7	14	21	28
Thursday	1	8	15	22	29
Friday	2	9	16	23	30
Saturday	3	10	17	24	31
Sunday	4	11	18	25	

SEPTEMBER
Monday		2	9	16	23
Tuesday		3	10	17	24
Wednesday		4	11	18	25
Thursday		5	12	19	26
Friday		6	13	20	27
Saturday		7	14	21	28
Sunday	1	8	15	22	29

OCTOBER
Monday	30	7	14	21	28
Tuesday	1	8	15	22	29
Wednesday	2	9	16	23	30
Thursday	3	10	17	24	31
Friday	4	11	18	25	
Saturday	5	12	19	26	
Sunday	6	13	20	27	

NOVEMBER
Monday		4	11	18	25
Tuesday		5	12	19	26
Wednesday		6	13	20	27
Thursday		7	14	21	28
Friday	1	8	15	22	29
Saturday	2	9	16	23	30
Sunday	3	10	17	24	

DECEMBER
Monday		2	9	16	23	
Tuesday		3	10	17	24	31
Wednesday		4	11	18	25	
Thursday		5	12	19	26	
Friday		6	13	20	27	
Saturday		7	14	21	28	
Sunday	1	8	15	22	29	

2020

JANUARY
Monday	30	6	13	20	27
Tuesday	31	7	14	21	28
Wednesday	1	8	15	22	29
Thursday	2	9	16	23	30
Friday	3	10	17	24	31
Saturday	4	11	18	25	
Sunday	5	12	19	26	

FEBRUARY
Monday		3	10	17	24
Tuesday		4	11	18	25
Wednesday		5	12	19	26
Thursday		6	13	20	27
Friday		7	14	21	28
Saturday	1	8	15	22	29
Sunday	2	9	16	23	

MARCH
Monday		2	9	16	23
Tuesday		3	10	17	24
Wednesday		4	11	18	25
Thursday		5	12	19	26
Friday		6	13	20	27
Saturday		7	14	21	28
Sunday	1	8	15	22	29

APRIL
Monday	30	6	13	20	27
Tuesday	31	7	14	21	28
Wednesday	1	8	15	22	29
Thursday	2	9	16	23	30
Friday	3	10	17	24	
Saturday	4	11	18	25	
Sunday	5	12	19	26	

MAY
Monday		4	11	18	25
Tuesday		5	12	19	26
Wednesday		6	13	20	27
Thursday		7	14	21	28
Friday	1	8	15	22	29
Saturday	2	9	16	23	30
Sunday	3	10	17	24	31

JUNE
Monday	1	8	15	22	29
Tuesday	2	9	16	23	30
Wednesday	3	10	17	24	
Thursday	4	11	18	25	
Friday	5	12	19	26	
Saturday	6	13	20	27	
Sunday	7	14	21	28	

JULY
Monday		6	13	20	27
Tuesday		7	14	21	28
Wednesday	1	8	15	22	29
Thursday	2	9	16	23	30
Friday	3	10	17	24	31
Saturday	4	11	18	25	
Sunday	5	12	19	26	

AUGUST
Monday		3	10	17	24
Tuesday		4	11	18	25
Wednesday		5	12	19	26
Thursday		6	13	20	27
Friday		7	14	21	28
Saturday	1	8	15	22	29
Sunday	2	9	16	23	30

SEPTEMBER
Monday	31	7	14	21	28
Tuesday	1	8	15	22	29
Wednesday	2	9	16	23	30
Thursday	3	10	17	24	
Friday	4	11	18	25	
Saturday	5	12	19	26	
Sunday	6	13	20	27	

OCTOBER
Monday		5	12	19	26
Tuesday		6	13	20	27
Wednesday		7	14	21	28
Thursday	1	8	15	22	29
Friday	2	9	16	23	30
Saturday	3	10	17	24	31
Sunday	4	11	18	25	

NOVEMBER
Monday		2	9	16	23
Tuesday		3	10	17	24
Wednesday		4	11	18	25
Thursday		5	12	19	26
Friday		6	13	20	27
Saturday		7	14	21	28
Sunday	1	8	15	22	29

DECEMBER
Monday	30	7	14	21	28
Tuesday	1	8	15	22	29
Wednesday	2	9	16	23	30
Thursday	3	10	17	24	31
Friday	4	11	18	25	
Saturday	5	12	19	26	
Sunday	6	13	20	27	

Edward Coley Burne-Jones *The Mermaid* 1882 Gouache and watercolour on paper 31.2 x 23.5 cm Tate. Bequeathed by Miss Katharine Elizabeth Lewis 1961

2019 YEAR PLANNER

JANUARY Monday	Tuesday	Wednesday	Thursday	Friday	Saturday	Sunday
	1	2	3	4	5	6
7	8	9	10	11	12	13
14	15	16	17	18	19	20
21	22	23	24	25	26	27
28	29	30	31			

FEBRUARY Monday	Tuesday	Wednesday	Thursday	Friday	Saturday	Sunday
				1	2	3
4	5	6	7	8	9	10
11	12	13	14	15	16	17
18	19	20	21	22	23	24
25	26	27	28			

MARCH Monday	Tuesday	Wednesday	Thursday	Friday	Saturday	Sunday
				1	2	3
4	5	6	7	8	9	10
11	12	13	14	15	16	17
18	19	20	21	22	23	24
25	26	27	28	29	30	31

APRIL

Monday	Tuesday	Wednesday	Thursday	Friday	Saturday	Sunday
1	2	3	4	5	6	7
8	9	10	11	12	13	14
15	16	17	18	19	20	21
22	23	24	25	26	27	28
29	30					

MAY

Monday	Tuesday	Wednesday	Thursday	Friday	Saturday	Sunday
		1	2	3	4	5
6	7	8	9	10	11	12
13	14	15	16	17	18	19
20	21	22	23	24	25	26
27	28	29	30	31		

JUNE

Monday	Tuesday	Wednesday	Thursday	Friday	Saturday	Sunday
					1	2
3	4	5	6	7	8	9
10	11	12	13	14	15	16
17	18	19	20	21	22	23
24	25	26	27	28	29	30

JULY

Monday	Tuesday	Wednesday	Thursday	Friday	Saturday	Sunday
1	2	3	4	5	6	7
8	9	10	11	12	13	14
15	16	17	18	19	20	21
22	23	24	25	26	27	28
29	30	31				

AUGUST / SEPTEMBER

Monday	Tuesday	Wednesday	Thursday	Friday	Saturday	Sunday
			1	2	3	4
5	6	7	8	9	10	11
12	13	14	15	16	17	18
19	20	21	22	23	24	25
26	27	28	29	30	31	1

SEPTEMBER

Monday	Tuesday	Wednesday	Thursday	Friday	Saturday	Sunday
2	3	4	5	6	7	8
9	10	11	12	13	14	15
16	17	18	19	20	21	22
23	24	25	26	27	28	29
30						

OCTOBER

Monday	Tuesday	Wednesday	Thursday	Friday	Saturday	Sunday
	1	2	3	4	5	6
7	8	9	10	11	12	13
14	15	16	17	18	19	20
21	22	23	24	25	26	27
28	29	30	31			

NOVEMBER / DECEMBER

Monday	Tuesday	Wednesday	Thursday	Friday	Saturday	Sunday
				1	2	3
4	5	6	7	8	9	10
11	12	13	14	15	16	17
18	19	20	21	22	23	24
25	26	27	28	29	30	1

DECEMBER

Monday	Tuesday	Wednesday	Thursday	Friday	Saturday	Sunday
2	3	4	5	6	7	8
9	10	11	12	13	14	15
16	17	18	19	20	21	22
23	24	25	26	27	28	29
30	31					

Edward Coley Burne-Jones
Love and the Pilgrim 1896-7
Oil paint on canvas
157.5 x 304.8 cm
Tate. Presented by the Art Fund 1942

JANUARY

31 Monday

1 Tuesday

2 Wednesday

3 Thursday

4 Friday

5 Saturday

6 Sunday

Monday		7	14	21	28
Tuesday	1	8	15	22	29
Wednesday	2	9	16	23	30
Thursday	3	10	17	24	31
Friday	4	11	18	25	
Saturday	5	12	19	26	
Sunday	6	13	20	27	

Dante Gabriel Rossetti
Monna Pomona 1864
Watercolour and gum arabic on paper
47.6 x 39.3 cm
Tate. Presented by Alfred A. de Pass 1910

JANUARY

7 Monday

8 Tuesday

9 Wednesday

10 Thursday

11 Friday

12 Saturday

13 Sunday

Monday		7	14	21	28
Tuesday	1	8	15	22	29
Wednesday	2	9	16	23	30
Thursday	3	10	17	24	31
Friday	4	11	18	25	
Saturday	5	12	19	26	
Sunday	6	13	20	27	

John Everett Millais
Miss Eveleen Tennant 1874
Oil paint on canvas
107.9 x 80 cm
Tate. Presented by Harold Myers 1941

JANUARY

14 Monday — 1975. Concert Cardiff

15 Tuesday

16 Wednesday

17 Thursday

18 Friday

19 Saturday — Jago and Jack's party.

20 Sunday

Monday		7	14	21	28
Tuesday	1	8	15	22	29
Wednesday	2	9	16	23	30
Thursday	3	10	17	24	31
Friday	4	11	18	25	
Saturday	5	12	19	26	
Sunday	6	13	20	27	

Edward Coley Burne-Jones
Desiderium 1873
Graphite on paper
21 x 13.3 cm
Tate. Presented by Sir Philip Burne-Jones Bt 1910

JANUARY

21 Monday

22 Tuesday

Cecilia's 18th Birthday!

23 Wednesday

24 Thursday

25 Friday

26 Saturday

27 Sunday

Monday		7	14	21	28
Tuesday	1	8	15	22	29
Wednesday	2	9	16	23	30
Thursday	3	10	17	24	31
Friday	4	11	18	25	
Saturday	5	12	19	26	
Sunday	6	13	20	27	

William Morris
La Belle Iseult 1858
Oil paint on canvas
71.8 x 50.2 cm
Tate. Bequeathed by Miss May Morris 1939

JANUARY / FEBRUARY

28 Monday

The Wombats. (concert)

29 Tuesday

30 Wednesday

31 Thursday

1 Friday

2 Saturday

3 Sunday

Monday		7	14	21	28
Tuesday	1	8	15	22	29
Wednesday	2	9	16	23	30
Thursday	3	10	17	24	31
Friday	4	11	18	25	
Saturday	5	12	19	26	
Sunday	6	13	20	27	

Edward Coley Burne-Jones
The Temple of Love
Oil paint on canvas
213.4 x 92.7 cm
Tate. Presented by the Trustees of the Chantrey Bequest 1919

FEBRUARY

4 Monday

5 Tuesday

6 Wednesday

7 Thursday

8 Friday — Babysitting (Sal + Chris)

9 Saturday

10 Sunday

Monday		4	11	18	25
Tuesday		5	12	19	26
Wednesday		6	13	20	27
Thursday		7	14	21	28
Friday	1	8	15	22	
Saturday	2	9	16	23	
Sunday	3	10	17	24	

Dante Gabriel Rossetti
Roman de la Rose 1864
Watercolour on paper
34.3 x 34.3 cm
Tate. Presented by Andrew Bain 1925

FEBRUARY

11 Monday

12 Tuesday

13 Wednesday

14 Thursday

15 Friday

16 Saturday

17 Sunday

Monday		4	11	18	25
Tuesday		5	12	19	26
Wednesday		6	13	20	27
Thursday		7	14	21	28
Friday	1	8	15	22	
Saturday	2	9	16	23	
Sunday	3	10	17	24	

Edward Coley Burne-Jones
Study of the Maid for 'King Cophetua and the Beggar Maid' 1883-4
Oil paint and drawing on paper
120.6 x 62.2 cm
Tate. Bequeathed by Miss Maud Beddington 1940

FEBRUARY

18 Monday

19 Tuesday

20 Wednesday

21 Thursday

22 Friday

23 Saturday

24 Sunday

Monday		4	11	18	25
Tuesday		5	12	19	26
Wednesday		6	13	20	27
Thursday		7	14	21	28
Friday	1	8	15	22	
Saturday	2	9	16	23	
Sunday	3	10	17	24	

Phillip Hermogenes Calderon
Broken Vows 1856
Oil paint on canvas
91.4 x 67.9 cm
Tate. Purchased 1947

FEBRUARY / MARCH

25 Monday

26 Tuesday

27 Wednesday

28 Thursday

1 Friday

2 Saturday

3 Sunday

Monday		4	11	18	25
Tuesday		5	12	19	26
Wednesday		6	13	20	27
Thursday		7	14	21	28
Friday	1	8	15	22	
Saturday	2	9	16	23	
Sunday	3	10	17	24	

John Singer Sargent
Carnation, Lily, Lily, Rose 1885–6
Oil paint on canvas
174 x 153.7 cm
Tate. Presented by the Trustees of the Chantrey Bequest 1887

MARCH

4 Monday

5 Tuesday

6 Wednesday

7 Thursday

8 Friday

9 Saturday

10 Sunday

Monday		4	11	18	25
Tuesday		5	12	19	26
Wednesday		6	13	20	27
Thursday		7	14	21	28
Friday	1	8	15	22	29
Saturday	2	9	16	23	30
Sunday	3	10	17	24	31

John Everett Millais
Christ in the House of His Parents ('The Carpenter's Shop') 1849-50
Oil paint on canvas
86.4 x 139.7 cm
Tate. Purchased with assistance from the Art Fund and various subscribers 1921

MARCH

11 Monday

12 Tuesday

13 Wednesday

14 Thursday

15 Friday

16 Saturday

17 Sunday

Monday		4	11	18	25
Tuesday		5	12	19	26
Wednesday		6	13	20	27
Thursday		7	14	21	28
Friday	1	8	15	22	29
Saturday	2	9	16	23	30
Sunday	3	10	17	24	31

Edward Coley Burne-Jones
The Mermaid 1882
Gouache and watercolour on paper
31.2 x 23.5 cm
Tate. Bequeathed by Miss Katharine Elizabeth Lewis 1961

MARCH

18 Monday

19 Tuesday

20 Wednesday

21 Thursday

22 Friday

23 Saturday

24 Sunday

Monday		4	11	18	25
Tuesday		5	12	19	26
Wednesday		6	13	20	27
Thursday		7	14	21	28
Friday	1	8	15	22	29
Saturday	2	9	16	23	30
Sunday	3	10	17	24	31

Dante Gabriel Rossetti
Beata Beatrix c.1864–70
Oil paint on canvas
86.4 x 66 cm
Tate. Presented by Georgiana Baroness Mount-Temple in memory of her husband, Francis, Baron Mount-Temple 1889

MARCH

25 Monday

26 Tuesday

27 Wednesday

28 Thursday

29 Friday

30 Saturday

31 Sunday

Monday		4	11	18	25
Tuesday		5	12	19	26
Wednesday		6	13	20	27
Thursday		7	14	21	28
Friday	1	8	15	22	29
Saturday	2	9	16	23	30
Sunday	3	10	17	24	31

Arthur Hughes
April Love 1855-6
Oil paint on canvas
88.9 x 49.5 cm
Tate. Purchased 1909

APRIL

1 Monday

2 Tuesday

3 Wednesday

4 Thursday

5 Friday

6 Saturday

7 Sunday

Monday	1	8	15	22	29
Tuesday	2	9	16	23	30
Wednesday	3	10	17	24	
Thursday	4	11	18	25	
Friday	5	12	19	26	
Saturday	6	13	20	27	
Sunday	7	14	21	28	

Dante Gabriel Rossetti
Ecce Ancilla Domini! (The Annunciation) 1849-50
Oil paint on canvas
72.4 x 41.9 cm
Tate. Purchased 1886

APRIL

8 Monday

9 Tuesday

10 Wednesday

11 Thursday

12 Friday

13 Saturday

14 Sunday

Monday	1	8	15	22	29
Tuesday	2	9	16	23	30
Wednesday	3	10	17	24	
Thursday	4	11	18	25	
Friday	5	12	19	26	
Saturday	6	13	20	27	
Sunday	7	14	21	28	

George Frederic Watts and assistants
Hope 1886
Oil paint on canvas
142.2 x 111.8 cm
Tate. Presented by George Frederic Watts 1897

APRIL

15 Monday

16 Tuesday

17 Wednesday

18 Thursday

19 Friday

20 Saturday

21 Sunday

Monday	1	8	15	22	29
Tuesday	2	9	16	23	30
Wednesday	3	10	17	24	
Thursday	4	11	18	25	
Friday	5	12	19	26	
Saturday	6	13	20	27	
Sunday	7	14	21	28	

John Roddam Spencer Stanhope
Thoughts of the Past exhibited 1859
Oil paint on canvas
86.4 x 50.8 cm
Tate. Presented by Mrs F. Evans 1918

APRIL

22 Monday

23 Tuesday

24 Wednesday

25 Thursday

26 Friday

27 Saturday

28 Sunday

Monday	1	8	15	22	29
Tuesday	2	9	16	23	30
Wednesday	3	10	17	24	
Thursday	4	11	18	25	
Friday	5	12	19	26	
Saturday	6	13	20	27	
Sunday	7	14	21	28	

Edward Coley Burne-Jones
The Golden Stairs 1880
Oil paint on canvas
269.2 x 116.8 cm
Tate. Bequeathed by Lord Battersea 1924

APRIL / MAY

29 Monday

30 Tuesday

1 Wednesday

2 Thursday

3 Friday

4 Saturday

5 Sunday

Monday	1	8	15	22	29
Tuesday	2	9	16	23	30
Wednesday	3	10	17	24	
Thursday	4	11	18	25	
Friday	5	12	19	26	
Saturday	6	13	20	27	
Sunday	7	14	21	28	

Dante Gabriel Rossetti
Sancta Lilias 1874
Oil paint on canvas
48.3 x 45.7 cm
Tate. Presented by Madame Deschamps in memory of Georgiana, Baroness Mount-Temple 1909

MAY

6 Monday

7 Tuesday

8 Wednesday

9 Thursday

10 Friday

11 Saturday

12 Sunday

Monday		6	13	20	27
Tuesday		7	14	21	28
Wednesday	1	8	15	22	29
Thursday	2	9	16	23	30
Friday	3	10	17	24	31
Saturday	4	11	18	25	
Sunday	5	12	19	26	

Edward Coley Burne-Jones
Study of a Girl's Head 1866
Graphite on paper
26 x 21.6 cm
Tate. Bequeathed by A.N. MacNicholl 1916

MAY

13 Monday

14 Tuesday

15 Wednesday

16 Thursday

17 Friday

18 Saturday

19 Sunday

Monday		6	13	20	27
Tuesday		7	14	21	28
Wednesday	1	8	15	22	29
Thursday	2	9	16	23	30
Friday	3	10	17	24	31
Saturday	4	11	18	25	
Sunday	5	12	19	26	

Dante Gabriel Rossetti
Lucrezia Borgia 1860-1
Graphite and watercolour on paper
43.8 x 25.8 cm
Tate. Presented in memory of Henry Michael Field by Charles Ricketts through the Art Fund 1916

MAY

20 Monday

21 Tuesday

22 Wednesday

23 Thursday

24 Friday

25 Saturday

26 Sunday

Monday		6	13	20	27
Tuesday		7	14	21	28
Wednesday	1	8	15	22	29
Thursday	2	9	16	23	30
Friday	3	10	17	24	31
Saturday	4	11	18	25	
Sunday	5	12	19	26	

John Everett Millais
Ophelia 1851-2
Oil paint on canvas
76.2 x 111.8 cm
Tate. Presented by Sir Henry Tate 1894

MAY / JUNE

27 Monday

28 Tuesday

29 Wednesday

30 Thursday

31 Friday

1 Saturday

2 Sunday

Monday		6	13	20	27
Tuesday		7	14	21	28
Wednesday	1	8	15	22	29
Thursday	2	9	16	23	30
Friday	3	10	17	24	31
Saturday	4	11	18	25	
Sunday	5	12	19	26	

Edward Coley Burne-Jones
Clara von Bork 1560 1860
Watercolour and gouache on paper
34.2 x 17.9 cm
Tate. Bequeathed by W. Graham Robertson 1948

JUNE

3 Monday

4 Tuesday

5 Wednesday

6 Thursday

7 Friday

8 Saturday
T & G
p 17
Brandenburg 5 I

9 Sunday
T & G p 18 P 6 I
+ P 34 Sonority Moyse + P 11
Nielsen Conc I 2A
Brandenburg 5 II + III

Monday		3	10	17	24
Tuesday		4	11	18	25
Wednesday		5	12	19	26
Thursday		6	13	20	27
Friday		7	14	21	28
Saturday	1	8	15	22	29
Sunday	2	9	16	23	30

John Frederick Lewis
Study for 'The Courtyard of the Coptic Patriarch's House in Cairo c. 1864
Oil paint on wood
36.8 x 35.6 cm
Tate. Purchased 1900

JUNE

10 Monday
Moyse Sonority
p6 1 p11 A2
p16 1 & 2
T & G p19
20 E & E No 1 Moyse

11 Tuesday
T & G p20
Sonority

12 Wednesday
Sonority
T & G p21
E & E·T No 1

13 Thursday

14 Friday

15 Saturday

16 Sunday

Monday		3	10	17	24
Tuesday		4	11	18	25
Wednesday		5	12	19	26
Thursday		6	13	20	27
Friday		7	14	21	28
Saturday	1	8	15	22	29
Sunday	2	9	16	23	30

Edward Coley Burne-Jones
Vespertina Quies 1893
Oil paint on canvas
107.9 x 62.2 cm
Tate. Bequeathed by Miss Maud Beddington 1940

JUNE

17 Monday

18 Tuesday

19 Wednesday

20 Thursday

21 Friday

22 Saturday

23 Sunday

Monday		3	10	17	24
Tuesday		4	11	18	25
Wednesday		5	12	19	26
Thursday		6	13	20	27
Friday		7	14	21	28
Saturday	1	8	15	22	29
Sunday	2	9	16	23	30

Theodor von Holst
The Bride 1842
Oil paint on canvas
92.3 x 71.3 cm
Tate. Presented by Tate Members 2015

JUNE

24 Monday

25 Tuesday

26 Wednesday

27 Thursday

28 Friday

29 Saturday

30 Sunday

Monday		3	10	17	24
Tuesday		4	11	18	25
Wednesday		5	12	19	26
Thursday		6	13	20	27
Friday		7	14	21	28
Saturday	1	8	15	22	29
Sunday	2	9	16	23	30

William Maw Egley
Omnibus Life in London 1859 (detail)
Oil paint on canvas
44.8 x 41.9 cm
Tate. Bequeathed by Miss J.L.R. Blaker 1947

JULY

1 Monday

2 Tuesday

3 Wednesday

4 Thursday

5 Friday

6 Saturday

7 Sunday

Monday	1	8	15	22	29
Tuesday	2	9	16	23	30
Wednesday	3	10	17	24	31
Thursday	4	11	18	25	
Friday	5	12	19	26	
Saturday	6	13	20	27	
Sunday	7	14	21	28	

Dante Gabriel Rossetti
The Girlhood of Mary Virgin 1848-9
Oil paint on canvas
83.2 x 65.4 cm
Tate. Bequeathed by Lady Jekyll 1937

JULY

8 Monday

9 Tuesday

10 Wednesday

11 Thursday

12 Friday

13 Saturday

14 Sunday

Monday	1	8	15	22	29
Tuesday	2	9	16	23	30
Wednesday	3	10	17	24	31
Thursday	4	11	18	25	
Friday	5	12	19	26	
Saturday	6	13	20	27	
Sunday	7	14	21	28	

John Everett Millais
The Boyhood of Raleigh 1870
Oil paint on canvas
120.6 x 142.2 cm
Tate. Presented by Amy, Lady Tate in memory of Sir Henry Tate 1900

JULY

15 Monday

16 Tuesday

17 Wednesday

18 Thursday

19 Friday

20 Saturday

21 Sunday

Monday	1	8	15	22	29
Tuesday	2	9	16	23	30
Wednesday	3	10	17	24	31
Thursday	4	11	18	25	
Friday	5	12	19	26	
Saturday	6	13	20	27	
Sunday	7	14	21	28	

Dante Gabriel Rossetti
The Beloved ('The Bride') 1865-6
Oil paint on canvas
82.5 x 76.2 cm
Tate. Purchased with assistance from Sir Arthur Du Cros Bt and Sir Otto Beit KCMG through the Art Fund 1916

JULY

22 Monday

23 Tuesday

24 Wednesday

25 Thursday

26 Friday

27 Saturday

28 Sunday

Monday	1	8	15	22	29
Tuesday	2	9	16	23	30
Wednesday	3	10	17	24	31
Thursday	4	11	18	25	
Friday	5	12	19	26	
Saturday	6	13	20	27	
Sunday	7	14	21	28	

Simeon Solomon
Sappho and Erinna in a Garden at Mytilene 1864
Watercolour on paper
33 x 38.1 cm
Tate. Purchased 1980

JULY / AUGUST

29 Monday

30 Tuesday

31 Wednesday

1 Thursday

2 Friday

3 Saturday

4 Sunday

Monday	1	8	15	22	29
Tuesday	2	9	16	23	30
Wednesday	3	10	17	24	31
Thursday	4	11	18	25	
Friday	5	12	19	26	
Saturday	6	13	20	27	
Sunday	7	14	21	28	

Edward Coley Burne-Jones
Summer Snow, engraved by the Dalziel Brothers pubished 1863
Wood engraving on paper
14.6 x 10.8 cm
Tate. Presented by Harold Hartley 1925

AUGUST

5 Monday

6 Tuesday

7 Wednesday

8 Thursday

9 Friday

10 Saturday

11 Sunday

Monday		5	12	19	26
Tuesday		6	13	20	27
Wednesday		7	14	21	28
Thursday	1	8	15	22	29
Friday	2	9	16	23	30
Saturday	3	10	17	24	31
Sunday	4	11	18	25	

Théodore Roussel
The Reading Girl 1886-7
Oil paint on canvas
152.4 x 161.3 cm
Tate. Presented by Mrs Walter Herriot and Miss R. Herriot in memory of the artist 1927

AUGUST

12 Monday

13 Tuesday

14 Wednesday

15 Thursday

16 Friday

17 Saturday

18 Sunday

Monday		5	12	19	26
Tuesday		6	13	20	27
Wednesday		7	14	21	28
Thursday	1	8	15	22	29
Friday	2	9	16	23	30
Saturday	3	10	17	24	31
Sunday	4	11	18	25	

Henry Wallis
Chatterton 1856
Oil paint on canvas
62.2 × 93.3 cm
Tate. Bequeathed by Charles Gent Clement 1899

AUGUST

19 Monday

20 Tuesday

21 Wednesday

22 Thursday

23 Friday

24 Saturday

25 Sunday

Monday		5	12	19	26
Tuesday		6	13	20	27
Wednesday		7	14	21	28
Thursday	1	8	15	22	29
Friday	2	9	16	23	30
Saturday	3	10	17	24	31
Sunday	4	11	18	25	

John Singer Sargent
Study of Mme Gautreau c.1884
Oil paint on canvas
206.4 x 107.9 cm
Tate. Presented by Lord Duveen through the Art Fund 1925

AUGUST / SEPTEMBER

26 Monday

27 Tuesday

28 Wednesday

29 Thursday

30 Friday

31 Saturday

1 Sunday

Monday		5	12	19	26
Tuesday		6	13	20	27
Wednesday		7	14	21	28
Thursday	1	8	15	22	29
Friday	2	9	16	23	30
Saturday	3	10	17	24	31
Sunday	4	11	18	25	

Dante Gabriel Rossetti
Proserpine 1874
Oil paint on canvas
125.1 x 61 cm
Tate. Presented by W. Graham Robertson 1940

SEPTEMBER

2 Monday

3 Tuesday

4 Wednesday

5 Thursday

6 Friday

7 Saturday

8 Sunday

Monday		2	9	16	23	30
Tuesday		3	10	17	24	
Wednesday		4	11	18	25	
Thursday		5	12	19	26	
Friday		6	13	20	27	
Saturday		7	14	21	28	
Sunday	1	8	15	22	29	

William Holman Hunt
The Awakening Conscience 1853
Oil paint on canvas
76.2 x 55.9 cm
Tate. Presented by Sir Colin and Lady Anderson through the Friends of the Tate Gallery 1976

SEPTEMBER

9 Monday

10 Tuesday

11 Wednesday

12 Thursday

13 Friday

14 Saturday

15 Sunday

Monday		2	9	16	23	30
Tuesday		3	10	17	24	
Wednesday		4	11	18	25	
Thursday		5	12	19	26	
Friday		6	13	20	27	
Saturday		7	14	21	28	
Sunday	1	8	15	22	29	

Dante Gabriel Rossetti
Paolo and Francesca da Rimini 1855
Watercolour on paper
25.4 x 44.9 cm
Tate. Purchased with assistance from Sir Arthur Du Cros Bt and Sir Otto Beit KCMG through the Art Fund 1916

SEPTEMBER

16 Monday

17 Tuesday

18 Wednesday

19 Thursday

20 Friday

21 Saturday

22 Sunday

Monday		2	9	16	23	30
Tuesday		3	10	17	24
Wednesday		4	11	18	25
Thursday		5	12	19	26
Friday		6	13	20	27
Saturday		7	14	21	28
Sunday	1	8	15	22	29

John Everett Millais
Mariana 1851
Oil paint on mahogany
59.7 x 49.5 cm
Tate. Accepted by HM Government in lieu of tax and allocated to the Tate Gallery 1999

SEPTEMBER

23 Monday

24 Tuesday

25 Wednesday

26 Thursday

27 Friday

28 Saturday

29 Sunday

Monday		2	9	16	23	30
Tuesday		3	10	17	24
Wednesday		4	11	18	25
Thursday		5	12	19	26
Friday		6	13	20	27
Saturday		7	14	21	28
Sunday	1	8	15	22	29

John William Waterhouse
The Lady of Shalott 1888
Oil paint on canvas
153 x 200 cm
Tate. Presented by Sir Henry Tate 1894

SEPTEMBER / OCTOBER

30 Monday

1 Tuesday

2 Wednesday

3 Thursday

4 Friday

5 Saturday

6 Sunday

Monday		7	14	21	28
Tuesday	1	8	15	22	29
Wednesday	2	9	16	23	30
Thursday	3	10	17	24	31
Friday	4	11	18	25	
Saturday	5	12	19	26	
Sunday	6	13	20	27	

John Singer Sargent
Ellen Terry as Lady Macbeth 1889
Oil paint on canvas
221 x 114.3 cm
Tate. Presented by Sir Joseph Duveen 1906

OCTOBER

7 Monday

8 Tuesday

9 Wednesday

10 Thursday

11 Friday

12 Saturday

13 Sunday

Monday		7	14	21	28
Tuesday	1	8	15	22	29
Wednesday	2	9	16	23	30
Thursday	3	10	17	24	31
Friday	4	11	18	25	
Saturday	5	12	19	26	
Sunday	6	13	20	27	

Dante Gabriel Rossetti
Monna Vanna 1866
Oil paint on canvas
88.9 x 86.4 cm
Tate. Purchased with assistance from Sir Arthur Du Cros Bt and Sir Otto Beit KCMG through the Art Fund 1916

OCTOBER

14 Monday

15 Tuesday

16 Wednesday

17 Thursday

18 Friday

19 Saturday

20 Sunday

Monday		7	14	21	28
Tuesday	1	8	15	22	29
Wednesday	2	9	16	23	30
Thursday	3	10	17	24	31
Friday	4	11	18	25	
Saturday	5	12	19	26	
Sunday	6	13	20	27	

Edward Coley Burne-Jones
Sidonia von Bork 1560 1860
Watercolour and gouache on paper
33.3 × 17.1 cm
Tate. Bequeathed by W. Graham Robertson 1948

OCTOBER

21 Monday

22 Tuesday

23 Wednesday

24 Thursday

25 Friday

26 Saturday

27 Sunday

Monday		7	14	21	28
Tuesday	1	8	15	22	29
Wednesday	2	9	16	23	30
Thursday	3	10	17	24	31
Friday	4	11	18	25	
Saturday	5	12	19	26	
Sunday	6	13	20	27	

William Blake Richmond
Portrait of Mrs Ernest Moon 1888
Oil paint on canvas
127.5 x 102 cm
Tate. Presented by the Patrons of British Art through the Tate Gallery Foundation 1996

OCTOBER / NOVEMBER

28 Monday

29 Tuesday

30 Wednesday

31 Thursday

1 Friday

2 Saturday

3 Sunday

Monday		7	14	21	28
Tuesday	1	8	15	22	29
Wednesday	2	9	16	23	30
Thursday	3	10	17	24	31
Friday	4	11	18	25	
Saturday	5	12	19	26	
Sunday	6	13	20	27	

John Brett
Lady with a Dove (Madame Loeser) 1864
Oil paint on canvas
61 x 45.7 cm
Tate. Presented by Lady Holroyd in accordance with the wishes of the late Sir Charles Holroyd 1919

NOVEMBER

4 Monday

5 Tuesday

6 Wednesday

7 Thursday

8 Friday

9 Saturday

10 Sunday

Monday		4	11	18	25
Tuesday		5	12	19	26
Wednesday		6	13	20	27
Thursday		7	14	21	28
Friday	1	8	15	22	29
Saturday	2	9	16	23	30
Sunday	3	10	17	24	

Edward Coley Burne-Jones
King Cophetua and the Beggar Maid 1884
Oil paint on canvas
293.4 x 135.9 cm
Tate. Presented by subscribers 1900

NOVEMBER

11 Monday

12 Tuesday

13 Wednesday

14 Thursday

15 Friday

16 Saturday

17 Sunday

Monday		4	11	18	25
Tuesday		5	12	19	26
Wednesday		6	13	20	27
Thursday		7	14	21	28
Friday	1	8	15	22	29
Saturday	2	9	16	23	30
Sunday	3	10	17	24	

John Everett Millais
Speak! Speak! 1895
Oil paint on canvas
167.6 x 210.8 cm
Tate. Presented by the Trustees of the Chantrey Bequest 1895

NOVEMBER

18 Monday

19 Tuesday

20 Wednesday

21 Thursday

22 Friday

23 Saturday

24 Sunday

Monday		4	11	18	25
Tuesday		5	12	19	26
Wednesday		6	13	20	27
Thursday		7	14	21	28
Friday	1	8	15	22	29
Saturday	2	9	16	23	30
Sunday	3	10	17	24	

William Holman Hunt
Portrait of Mrs Edith Holman Hunt 1880
Chalk and pastel on paper
42.8 x 33.8 cm
Tate. Presented by Arthur and Helen Grogan through the Art Fund 2009

NOVEMBER / DECEMBER

25 Monday

26 Tuesday

27 Wednesday

28 Thursday

29 Friday

30 Saturday

1 Sunday

Monday		4	11	18	25
Tuesday		5	12	19	26
Wednesday		6	13	20	27
Thursday		7	14	21	28
Friday	1	8	15	22	29
Saturday	2	9	16	23	30
Sunday	3	10	17	24	

Dante Gabriel Rossetti
Aurelia (Fazio's Mistress) 1863-1873
Oil paint on mahogany
43.2 x 36.8 cm
Tate. Purchased with assistance from Sir Arthur Du Cros Bt and Sir Otto Beit KCMG through the Art Fund 1916

DECEMBER

2 Monday

3 Tuesday

4 Wednesday

5 Thursday

6 Friday

7 Saturday

8 Sunday

Monday		2	9	16	23	30
Tuesday		3	10	17	24	31
Wednesday		4	11	18	25	
Thursday		5	12	19	26	
Friday		6	13	20	27	
Saturday		7	14	21	28	
Sunday	1	8	15	22	29	

John William Waterhouse
Saint Eulalia exhibited 1885
Oil paint on canvas
188.6 x 117.5 cm
Tate. Presented by Sir Henry Tate 1894

DECEMBER

9 Monday

10 Tuesday

11 Wednesday

12 Thursday

13 Friday

14 Saturday

15 Sunday

Monday		2	9	16	23	30
Tuesday		3	10	17	24	31
Wednesday		4	11	18	25	
Thursday		5	12	19	26	
Friday		6	13	20	27	
Saturday		7	14	21	28	
Sunday	1	8	15	22	29	

Thomas Copper Gotch
Alleluia exhibited 1896
Oil paint on canvas
133.3 x 184.1 cm
Tate. Presented by the Trustees of the Chantrey Bequest 1896

DECEMBER

16 Monday

17 Tuesday

18 Wednesday

19 Thursday

20 Friday

21 Saturday

22 Sunday

Monday		2	9	16	23	30
Tuesday		3	10	17	24	31
Wednesday		4	11	18	25	
Thursday		5	12	19	26	
Friday		6	13	20	27	
Saturday		7	14	21	28	
Sunday	1	8	15	22	29	

Edward Coley Burne-Jones
The Annunciation and the Adoration of the Magi 1861 (detail)
Oil paint on three canvases
108.6 x 73.7 cm, 108.6 x 156.2 cm, 108.6 x 73.7 cm
Tate. Presented by G.H. Bodley in memory of George Frederick Bodley 1934

DECEMBER

23 Monday

24 Tuesday

25 Wednesday

26 Thursday

27 Friday

28 Saturday

29 Sunday

Monday		2	9	16	23	30
Tuesday		3	10	17	24	31
Wednesday		4	11	18	25	
Thursday		5	12	19	26	
Friday		6	13	20	27	
Saturday		7	14	21	28	
Sunday	1	8	15	22	29	

Dante Gabriel Rossetti
Dantis Amor 1860
Oil paint on mahogany
74.9 x 81.3 cm
Tate. Presented by F. Treharne James 1920

DECEMBER / JANUARY

30 Monday

31 Tuesday

1 Wednesday

2 Thursday

3 Friday

4 Saturday

5 Sunday

Monday		2	9	16	23	30
Tuesday		3	10	17	24	31
Wednesday		4	11	18	25	
Thursday		5	12	19	26	
Friday		6	13	20	27	
Saturday		7	14	21	28	
Sunday	1	8	15	22	29	

NAMES AND ADDRESSES

Name:		Name:	
Address		Address	
Home Phone		Home Phone	
Mobile		Mobile	
Email		Email	
Name:		Name:	
Address		Address	
Home Phone		Home Phone	
Mobile		Mobile	
Email		Email	
Name:		Name:	
Address		Address	
Home Phone		Home Phone	
Mobile		Mobile	
Email		Email	

NAMES AND ADDRESSES

Name:		Name:	
Address		Address	
Home Phone		Home Phone	
Mobile		Mobile	
Email		Email	
Name:		Name:	
Address		Address	
Home Phone		Home Phone	
Mobile		Mobile	
Email		Email	
Name:		Name:	
Address		Address	
Home Phone		Home Phone	
Mobile		Mobile	
Email		Email	

NAMES AND ADDRESSES

Name:		Name:	
Address		Address	
Home Phone		Home Phone	
Mobile		Mobile	
Email		Email	
Name:		Name:	
Address		Address	
Home Phone		Home Phone	
Mobile		Mobile	
Email		Email	
Name:		Name:	
Address		Address	
Home Phone		Home Phone	
Mobile		Mobile	
Email		Email	

NAMES AND ADDRESSES

Name:		Name:	
Address		Address	
Home Phone		Home Phone	
Mobile		Mobile	
Email		Email	
Name:		Name:	
Address		Address	
Home Phone		Home Phone	
Mobile		Mobile	
Email		Email	
Name:		Name:	
Address		Address	
Home Phone		Home Phone	
Mobile		Mobile	
Email		Email	

NAMES AND ADDRESSES

Name:		Name:	
Address		Address	
Home Phone		Home Phone	
Mobile		Mobile	
Email		Email	
Name:		Name:	
Address		Address	
Home Phone		Home Phone	
Mobile		Mobile	
Email		Email	
Name:		Name:	
Address		Address	
Home Phone		Home Phone	
Mobile		Mobile	
Email		Email	

NAMES AND ADDRESSES

Name:		Name:	
Address		Address	
Home Phone		Home Phone	
Mobile		Mobile	
Email		Email	
Name:		Name:	
Address		Address	
Home Phone		Home Phone	
Mobile		Mobile	
Email		Email	
Name:		Name:	
Address		Address	
Home Phone		Home Phone	
Mobile		Mobile	
Email		Email	

NAMES AND ADDRESSES

Name:		Name:	
Address		Address	
Home Phone		Home Phone	
Mobile		Mobile	
Email		Email	
Name:		Name:	
Address		Address	
Home Phone		Home Phone	
Mobile		Mobile	
Email		Email	
Name:		Name:	
Address		Address	
Home Phone		Home Phone	
Mobile		Mobile	
Email		Email	

NAMES AND ADDRESSES

Name:		Name:	
Address		Address	
Home Phone		Home Phone	
Mobile		Mobile	
Email		Email	
Name:		Name:	
Address		Address	
Home Phone		Home Phone	
Mobile		Mobile	
Email		Email	
Name:		Name:	
Address		Address	
Home Phone		Home Phone	
Mobile		Mobile	
Email		Email	

NAMES AND ADDRESSES

Name:		Name:	
Address		Address	
Home Phone		Home Phone	
Mobile		Mobile	
Email		Email	
Name:		Name:	
Address		Address	
Home Phone		Home Phone	
Mobile		Mobile	
Email		Email	
Name:		Name:	
Address		Address	
Home Phone		Home Phone	
Mobile		Mobile	
Email		Email	

NAMES AND ADDRESSES

Name:		Name:	
Address		Address	
Home Phone		Home Phone	
Mobile		Mobile	
Email		Email	
Name:		Name:	
Address		Address	
Home Phone		Home Phone	
Mobile		Mobile	
Email		Email	
Name:		Name:	
Address		Address	
Home Phone		Home Phone	
Mobile		Mobile	
Email		Email	

NAMES AND ADDRESSES

Name:		Name:	
Address		Address	
Home Phone		Home Phone	
Mobile		Mobile	
Email		Email	
Name:		Name:	
Address		Address	
Home Phone		Home Phone	
Mobile		Mobile	
Email		Email	
Name:		Name:	
Address		Address	
Home Phone		Home Phone	
Mobile		Mobile	
Email		Email	

NAMES AND ADDRESSES

Name:		Name:	
Address		Address	
Home Phone		Home Phone	
Mobile		Mobile	
Email		Email	
Name:		Name:	
Address		Address	
Home Phone		Home Phone	
Mobile		Mobile	
Email		Email	
Name:		Name:	
Address		Address	
Home Phone		Home Phone	
Mobile		Mobile	
Email		Email	

NOTES

NOTES

NOTES

NOTES

NOTES

NOTES

NOTES

NOTES

PRINCIPAL REGIONAL GALLERIES

ENGLAND

Bedford
The Higgins Bedford
Castle Lane, Bedford MK40 3XD
T: 0123 4718 6181
www.thehigginsbedford.org.uk

Birmingham
The Barber Institute of Fine Arts
University of Birmingham
Edgbaston, Birmingham B15 2TS
T: 0121 414 7333
www.barber.org.uk
Birmingham Museum and Art Gallery
Chamberlain Square
Birmingham B3 3DH
T: 0121 303 1966
www.bmag.org.uk
Ikon Gallery
1 Oozells Square
Birmingham B1 2HS
T: 0121 248 0708
www.ikon-gallery.org

Bolton
Bolton Museum Art Gallery and Aquarium
Le Mans Crescent
Bolton BL1 1SE
T: 01204 332 211
www.boltonmuseums.org.uk

Bradford
Cartwright Hall Art Gallery
Lister Park, Bradford BD9 4NS
T: 01274 431 212
www.bradfordmuseums.org

Brighton
Brighton Museum and Art Gallery
Royal Pavilion Gardens
Brighton, E. Sussex BN1 1EE
T: 0300 029 0900
www.brighton-hove-rpml.org.uk

Bristol
Arnolfini
16 Narrow Quay, Bristol BS1 4QA
T: 0117 917 2300
www.arnolfini.org.uk
City of Bristol Museum and Art Gallery
Queen's Road, Bristol BS8 1RL
T: 0117 922 3571
www.bristol-city.gov.uk/museums

Cambridge
Fitzwilliam Museum
Trumpington Street,
Cambridge CB2 1RB
T: 01223 332 900
www.fitzmuseum.cam.ac.uk
Kettle's Yard
Castle Street, Cambridge CB3 0AQ
T: 01223 748 100
www.kettlesyard.co.uk

Chichester
Cass Sculpture Foundation
Sculpture Estate
New Barn Hill
Goodwood, Chichester
W. Sussex PO18 0QP
T: 01243 538 449
www.sculpture.org.uk

Compton
Watts Gallery
Down Lane, Compton
Guildford, Surrey GU3 1DQ
T: 01483 810235
www.wattsgallery.org.uk

Compton Verney
Compton Verney House
Warwickshire CV35 9HZ
T: 01926 645 500
www.comptonverney.org.uk

Cookham-on-Thames
Stanley Spencer Gallery
The King's Hall, High Street
Cookham, Berkshire SL6 9SJ
T: 01628 471 885
www.stanleyspencer.org.uk

Gateshead
Baltic – The Centre for Contemporary Art
Gateshead Quays
South Shore Road
Gateshead NE8 3BA
T: 0191 478 1810
www.balticmill.com
Shipley Art Gallery
Prince Consort Road
Gateshead NE8 4JB
T: 0191 477 1495
www.twmuseums.org.uk/shipley-art-gallery

Hull
Ferens Art Gallery
Little Queen Street
Hull HU1 3RA
T: 01482 613 902
www.hullcc.gov.uk/museums

Ipswich
Christchurch Mansion
Christchurch Park
Soane Street, Ipswich
Suffolk IP4 2BE
T: 01473 433 554
www.cimuseums.org.uk/venues/christchurch-mansion

Kendal
Abbot Hall Art Gallery
Kirkland, Kendal, Cumbria
LA9 5AL
T: 01539 722 464
www.abbothall.org.uk

Leeds
Henry Moore Institute
74 The Headrow, Leeds LS1 3AH
T: 0113 246 7467
www.henry-moore.org/hmi
Leeds City Art Gallery
The Headrow, Leeds LS1 3AA
T: 0113 247 8256
www.leeds.gov.uk/artgallery

Liverpool
Lady Lever Art Gallery
Port Sunlight Village
Wirral CH62 5EQ
T: 0151 478 4136
www.liverpoolmuseums.org.uk/ladylever
Sudley House
Mossley Hill Road, Aigburth
Liverpool L18 8BX
T: 0151 724 3245
www.liverpoolmuseums.org.uk/sudley
Tate Liverpool
Albert Dock, Liverpool L3 4BB
T: 0151 702 7400
www.tate.org.uk/liverpool
Walker Art Gallery
William Brown Street
Liverpool L3 8EL
T: 0151 478 4199
www.liverpoolmuseums.org.uk/walker

Manchester
Cornerhouse
70 Oxford Street
Manchester M1 5NH
T: 0161 200 1500
www.cornerhouse.org
Imperial War Museum North
The Quays, Trafford Wharf
Trafford Park
Manchester M17 1TZ
T: 0161 836 4000
www.iwm.org.uk/north
Manchester Art Gallery
Mosley Street
Manchester M3 3JL
T: 0161 235 8888
www.manchestergalleries.org
The Whitworth Art Gallery
The University of Manchester
Oxford Road
Manchester M15 6ER
T: 0161 275 7450
www.whitworth.manchester.ac.uk

Margate
Turner Contemporary
The Rendezvous
Margate, Kent CT9 1HG
T: 01843 233 000
www.turnercontemporary.org

Milton Keynes
Milton Keynes Gallery
900 Midsummer Boulevard
Central Milton Keynes MK9 3QA
T: 01908 676 900
www.mkgallery.org

Much Hadham
The Henry Moore Foundation
Dane Tree House, Perry Green
Much Hadham
Hertfordshire SG10 6EE
T: 01279 843 333

Newcastle upon Tyne
Laing Art Gallery
New Bridge Street
Newcastle upon Tyne NE1 8AG
T: 0191 232 7734
www.twmuseums.org.uk/laing

Norwich
Norwich Castle Museum and Art Gallery
Castle Hill, Norwich NR1 3JU
T: 01603 493 649
www.museums.norfolk.gov.uk
Sainsbury Centre for Visual Arts
University of East Anglia
Norwich NR4 7TJ
T: 01603 593 199
www.scva.org.uk

Oxford
Ashmolean Museum
Beaumont Street, Oxford OX1 2PH
T: 01865 278 002
www.ashmolean.org
Modern Art Oxford
30 Pembroke Street,
Oxford OX1 1BP
T: 01865 722 733
www.modernartoxford.org.uk

St Ives
Barbara Hepworth Museum & Sculpture Garden
Barnoon Hill, St Ives
Cornwall TR26 1AD
T: 01736 796 226
www.tate.org.uk/stives/hepworth
Tate St Ives
Porthmeor Beach, St Ives
Cornwall TR26 1TG
T: 01736 796 226
www.tate.org.uk/stives

Salford
The Lowry
Pier 8, Salford Quays
Greater Manchester M50 3AZ
T: 0843 208 6000
www.thelowry.com
Salford Museum and Art Gallery
Peel Park, The Crescent, Salford
Greater Manchester M5 4WU
T: 0161 778 0800
www.salfordmuseum.gov.uk

Salisbury
New Art Centre
Roche Court, East Winterslow
Salisbury, Wiltshire SP5 1BG
T: 01980 862244
www.sculpture.uk.com

Sheffield
Graves Art Gallery
Surrey Street, Sheffield,
South Yorkshire S1 2LH
T: 0114 278 2600
www.museums-sheffield.org.uk
Millennium Galleries
Arundel Gate, Sheffield S1 2PP
T: 0114 278 2600
www.museums-sheffield.org.uk
Weston Park Museum
Weston Park, Sheffield S10 2TP
T: 0114 278 2600
www.museums-sheffield.org.uk

Southampton
Southampton City Art Gallery
Civic Centre, Commercial Road
Southampton SO14 7LP
T: 023 8083 2277
www.southampton.gov.uk/art

Sudbury
Gainsborough's House
46-47 Gainsborough Street
Sudbury, Suffolk CO10 2EU
T: 01787 372 958
www.gainsborough.org

Wakefield
The Hepworth Wakefield
Gallery Walk
Wakefield WF1 5AW
T: 01924 247 360
www.hepworthwakefield.org
Yorkshire Sculpture Park
West Bretton
Wakefield WF4 4LG
T: 01924 832 631
www.ysp.co.uk

Walsall
New Art Gallery Walsall
Gallery Square, Walsall WS2 8LG
T: 01922 654 400
www.artatwalsall.org.uk

York
York Art Gallery
Exhibition Square, York YO1 7EW
T: 01904 687 687
www.yorkartgallery.org.uk

NORTHERN IRELAND

Belfast
Ulster Museum
Botanic Gardens
Belfast
BT9 5AB
T: 0845 608 0000
www.ulstermuseum.org.uk

SCOTLAND

Aberdeen
Aberdeen Art Gallery
Schoolhill, Aberdeen AB10 1FQ
T: 01224 523 700
www.aagm.co.uk

Dundee
Dundee Contemporary Arts
152 Nethergate
Dundee DD1 4DY
T: 01382 909 900
www.dca.org.uk

Edinburgh
City Art Centre
2 Market Street
Edinburgh EH1 1DE
T: 0131 529 3993 www.edinburghmuseums.org.uk
The Dean Gallery
73 Belford Road
Edinburgh EH4 3DS
T: 0131 624 6200
www.nationalgalleries.org
The Fruitmarket Gallery
45 Market Street
Edinburgh EH1 1DF
T: 0131 225 2383
www.fruitmarket.co.uk

National Gallery of Scotland
The Mound
Edinburgh EH2 2EL
T: 0131 624 6200
www.nationalgalleries.org
Scottish National Gallery of Modern Art
75 Belford Road
Edinburgh EH4 3DR
T: 0131 624 6558
www.nationalgalleries.org
Scottish National Portrait Gallery
1 Queen Street
Edinburgh EH2 1JD
T: 0131 624 6200
www.nationalgalleries.org

Glasgow
Burrell Collection
Pollok Country Park
2060 Pollokshaws Road
Glasgow
Strathclyde G43 1AT
T: 0141 287 2550
www.glasgowlife.org.uk
Centre for Contemporary Art
350 Sauchiehall Street
Glasgow G2 3JD
T: 0141 352 4900
www.cca-glasgow.com
Gallery of Modern Art
Royal Exchange Square
Glasgow G1 3AH
T: 0141 287 3050
www.glasgowlife.org.uk

WALES

Cardiff
National Museums and Galleries of Wales
Cathays Park, Cardiff CF10 3NP
T: 029 2057 3000
www.museumwales.ac.uk

Swansea
Glynn Vivian Art Gallery
Alexandra Road
Swansea SA1 5DZ
T: 01792 516 900
www.glynnvivian.com

LONDON MUSEUMS AND GALLERIES

Barbican Art Gallery
Barbican Centre, Silk Street
London EC2Y 8DS
T: 020 7638 4141
www.barbican.org.uk/art-gallery

The British Library
96 Euston Road
London NW1 2DB
T: 0843 208 1144
www.bl.uk

The British Museum
Great Russell Street
London WC1B 3DG
T: 020 7323 8299
www.britishmuseum.org

Camden Arts Centre
Arkwright Road
London NW3 6DG
T: 020 7472 5500
www.camdenartscentre.org

Churchill Museum &
Cabinet War Rooms
Clive Steps
King Charles Street
London SW1A 2AQ
T: 020 7930 6961
www.iwm.org.uk/visits/churchill-war-rooms

The Courtauld Institute of Art
Somerset House, Strand
London WC2R 0RN
T: 020 7872 0220
www.courtauld.ac.uk

Crafts Council
44a Pentonville Road
London N1 9BY
T: 020 7806 2500
www.craftscouncil.org.uk

Design Museum
28 Shad Thames
London SE1 2YD
T: 020 7403 6933
www.designmuseum.org

Dulwich Picture Gallery
Gallery Road, Dulwich
London SE21 7AD
T: 020 8693 5254
www.dulwichpicturegallery.org.uk

Geffrye Museum
136 Kingsland Road
London E2 8EA
T: 020 7739 9893
www.geffrye-museum.org.uk

Hayward Gallery
Southbank Centre
Belvedere Road
London SE1 8XX
T: 020 7960 4200
www.southbankcentre.co.uk/venues/hayward-gallery

Hogarth's House
Hogarth Lane
Great West Road, Chiswick
London W4 2QN
T: 020 8994 6757
www.hounslow.info/arts/hogarthshouse

Horniman Museum
100 London Road, Forest Hill
London SE23 3PQ
T: 020 8699 1872
www.horniman.ac.uk

Hunterian Museum
35-43 Lincoln's Inn Fields
London WC2A 3PE
T: 020 7869 6560
www.rcseng.ac.uk/museums/hunterian

Imperial War Museum
Lambeth Road
London SE1 6HZ
T: 020 7416 5320
www.iwm.org.uk

Institute of
Contemporary Arts
The Mall
London SW1Y 5AH
T: 020 7930 3647
www.ica.org.uk

Kenwood House
Hampstead Lane
London NW3 7JR
T: 0870 333 1181
www.english-heritage.org.uk

Jewish Museum
129–131 Albert Street
London NW1 7NB
T: 020 7284 7384
www.jewishmuseum.org.uk

Kensington Palace
Kensington Gardens
London W8 4PX
T: 0844 482 7777
www.hrp.org.uk

Leighton House Museum
12 Holland Park Road
London W14 8LZ
T: 020 7602 3316
www.rbkc.gov.uk/leightonhousemuseums

London Transport Museum
Covent Garden Piazza
London WC2E 7BB
T: 020 7379 6344
www.ltmuseum.co.uk

Museum of London
150 London Wall
London EC2Y 5HN
T: 020 7001 9844
www.museumoflondon.org.uk

The National Archives
Kew, Richmond
Surrey TW9 4DU
T: 020 8876 3444
www.nationalarchives.gov.uk

The National Gallery
Trafalgar Square
London WC2N 5DN
T: 020 7747 2885
www.nationalgallery.org.uk

National Maritime Museum
Romney Road, Greenwich
London SE10 9NF
T: 020 8858 4422
www.rmg.co.uk

National Portrait Gallery
St Martin's Place
London WC2H 0HE
T: 020 7306 0055
www.npg.org.uk

Natural History Museum
Cromwell Road
London SW7 5BD
T: 020 7942 5000
www.nhm.ac.uk

Petrie Museum of Egyptian
Archaeology
University College London
Malet Place
Gower Street
London WC1E 6BT
T: 020 7679 2884
www.ucl.ac.uk/museums/
petrie

The Photographers' Gallery
16–18 Ramillies Street
W1F 7LW
T: 020 7087 9300
www.thephotographersgallery.org.uk

The Queen's Gallery
Buckingham Palace
London SW1A 1AA
T: 020 7766 7300
www.royalcollection.org,uk

Royal Academy of Arts
Burlington House
Piccadilly
London W1J 0BD
T: 020 7300 8000
www.royalacademy.org.uk

Royal Armouries
HM Tower of London
London EC3N 4AB
T: 020 3166 6660
www.royalarmouries.org

Royal College of Art
Kensington Gore
London SW7 2EU
T: 020 7590 4444
www.rca.ac.uk

Saatchi Gallery
Duke of York Headquarters
Kings Road
London SW3 4RY
T: 020 7811 3070
www.saatchi-gallery.com

Science Museum
Exhibition Road
South Kensington
London SW7 2DD
T: 0870 870 4868
www.sciencemuseum.org.uk

Serpentine Gallery
Kensington Gardens
London W2 3XA
T: 020 7402 6075
www.serpentinegalleries.org

Serpentine Sackler Gallery
West Carriage Drive
London W2 2AR
T: 020 7402 6075
www.serpentinegalleries.org

Sir John Soane's Museum
13 Lincoln's Inn Fields
London WC2A 3BP
T: 020 7405 2107
www.soane.org

Tate Britain
Millbank
London SW1P 4RG
T: 020 7887 8888
www.tate.org.uk/britain

Tate Modern
Bankside
London SE1 9TG
T: 020 7887 8888
www.tate.org.uk/modern

Victoria and Albert Museum
Cromwell Road
London SW7 2RL
T: 020 7942 2000
www.vam.ac.uk

V&A Museum of Childhood
Cambridge Heath Road
London E2 9PA
T: 020 8983 5200
www.museumofchildhood.org.uk

Wallace Collection
Hertford House
Manchester Square
London W1U 3BN
T: 020 7563 9500
www.wallacecollection.org

Wellcome Collection
183 Euston Rd
London NW1 2BE
T: 020 7611 2222
www.wellcomecollection.org

Whitechapel Gallery
77–82 Whitechapel High Street
London E1 7QX
T: 020 7522 7888
www.whitechapelgallery.org

William Morris Gallery
Lloyd Park
Forest Road, Walthamstow
London E17 4PP
T: 020 8496 3000
www.walthamforest.gov.uk/williammorris

SUPPORTING TATE

Tate relies on a large number of supporters – individuals, foundations, companies and public sector sources – to enable us to deliver our world-class programme of activities. This support is essential for us to be able to acquire works of art for the collection, run education, outreach and exhibition programmes, care for the collection and enable art to be displayed, both digitally and physically, inside and outside Tate.

Your donation will make a real difference to our work and enable others to enjoy Tate and its collection both now and in the future. There are a variety of ways in which you can help support Tate.

TATE PATRONS
Tate Patrons share a strong enthusiasm for art and are committed to giving financial support to Tate on an annual basis. Support from Patrons provides much needed funding for acquisitions, exhibitions, conservation and education projects, which are at the heart of Tate endeavours. By continuing to give every year, Patrons become closely engaged in the life of Tate and are able to share their interest in art in an enjoyable and stimulating environment.

CORPORATE MEMBERSHIP
Corporate Membership at Tate Britain, Tate Liverpool and Tate Modern offers companies opportunities for corporate entertaining and the chance for a wide variety of employee benefits. These include special private views, special access to paying exhibitions, out-of-hours visits and tours, invitations to VIP events and talks at Members' offices.

CORPORATE INVESTMENT
Tate has developed a number of imaginative partnerships with the corporate sector, ranging from international interpretation and exhibition programmes to local outreach and staff development programmes. We are particularly known for our high-profile business marketing initiatives and employee benefit packages.

TATE ANNUAL FUND
A donation to the Annual Fund provides unrestricted support to the gallery, helping to make possible Tate's educational programmes and the care, study and exhibition of our unparalleled collection.

LEGACIES
A legacy can help secure Tate's future and may take the form of a residual share of an estate, a specific cash sum or item of property such as a work of art. Legacies to Tate are free of Inheritance Tax and help to secure a strong future for the collection and galleries.

OFFERS IN LIEU OF TAX
Inheritance Tax can be satisfied by transferring to the government a work of art of outstanding importance. In this case the rate of tax is reduced, and it can be made a condition of the offer that the work of art is allocated to Tate.

GIFTS OF SHARES
All gifts of quoted shares and securities are exempt from Capital Gains Tax. For higher-rate taxpayers, a gift of shares saves Income Tax as well as Capital Gains Tax.

AMERICAN PATRONS OF TATE
American Patrons of Tate is an independent charity based in New York that supports the work of Tate in the United Kingdom. It receives full tax-exempt status from the IRS under section 501 (c) (3), allowing United States taxpayers to receive tax deductions on gifts towards annual membership programs, exhibitions, scholarship and capital projects. For more information please contact the American Patrons of Tate office at American Patrons of Tate, 1285 6th Avenue (35th floor), New York, NY 10019, USA.
Tel: 001 212 882 5119/Fax: 001 212 882 5571.

To support Tate and for further information please contact us at:

Development Office
Tate, Millbank
London SW1P 4RG
Tel: 020 7887 8945/Fax: 020 7887 8098

ISBN: 978-1-84976-609-8

© Tate 2018. All rights reserved

Designed by Tate Enterprises Ltd
Photography by Tate Photography
Published in 2018 by Tate Enterprises Ltd Millbank,
London SW1P 4RG
www.tate.org.uk/publishing

Printed in China

Cover:
Edward Coley Burne-Jones
The Golden Stairs
Oil paint on canvas
29.2 x 116.8 cm
Tate. Bequeathed by Lord Battersea 1924

All holiday dates correct at time of press

Every effort has been made to contact the copyright
holders of the works reproduced. The publishers apologise
for any omissions that may inadvertently have been made.